DEDICATION

TO:

FROM:

May the love of all humanity
fill your path
and fulfill your life
with a succession of
successful successes.

Meher D. Amalsad

Copyright © 1996 by Meher Amalsad

All rights reserved. Printed and published in the United States of America. No part of this publication may be reproduced or distributed in any form or by any means without the prior written permission of the author, except in the case of quotations embodied in critical articles and reviews.

Library of Congress Catalog Card Number
96-096132

International Standard Book Number
1-888912-02-2

Second Edition

Gifts That Lift
Shift & Uplift

Words You Can Share,
With People Who Care

By
Meher D. Amalsad
©1996

What Others Are Saying About Meher Amalsad...

"Meher, your inspiring presentation about unconditional love brought tears to my eyes. As you reach many people, you will truly touch their hearts. Thank you for contributing to the creation of an enlightened planetary civilization."
Dr. Theresa Dale, Ph.D., ND., President and Founder of The Wellness Center for Research and Education Inc.

"Your informative, educational and motivational presentation 'In Search of Your Quest, How To Do Your Best,' undoubtedly left a positive impression on our members. In addition, the audience participation in your inspirational song, 'Success With Dreams' was truly overwhelming. Thank you for your commitment to success."
Barrett Van Buren, Director of Placement, ITT Corporation

"Meher's insights into the power of unconditional love will serve as guideposts for any person, business or school, wishing to add more depth, meaning and blessing to their personal relationships."
Jack Schlatter, Professional Speaker, Humorist and Author, Gifts by the Side of the Road

"Meher is an impassioned speaker who knows his quest and is willing to share it with his audiences so that they too will find self-empowerment and fulfillment."
R. Gregory Alonzo, Author, Say Yes To Success

"In your presentation 'Love Grows and Shows Only if it Flows,' you truly enlightened our lives by sharing some extra-ordinary experiences of unconditional love with your daughter Anahita. Your message of treating people as Human Beings instead of Human Doings was striking to the mind, vitalizing to the body and appealing to the soul."
Del Fox, Program Chairman, The Rotary Club

"Meher Amalsad is unique. I have had the distinctive privilege of knowing Meher in both his personal and professional persona. He is exactly what he seems to be... highly intelligent, value oriented and caring for others. As a connoisseur of motivational speakers, I rank Meher in the top 1%. His optimistic and unconditional concern for others differentiates hem from the usual 'What's in it for me' message of other well known speakers."
Pat Gammon, Division Manager, ICM SunAmerica Securities, Inc.

Gifts That Lift *Shift* & Uplift

Words You Can Share, With People Who Care

This book contains excerpts from Meher Amalsad's two new books and audio programs
IN SEARCH OF YOUR QUEST
HOW TO DO YOUR BEST
&
LOVE GROWS AND SHOWS
ONLY IF IT FLOWS

The quotes in this book reflect a life-time of experiences in caring, sharing, living and loving humanity.

Acknowledgments

First and foremost, I would like to thank God for giving me the inspiration to write this book.

Next to God, I would like to thank my wife, Katayoon and my daughter Anahita for their continuing support, especially during the time I spent at home in compiling the information for this book.

I would also like to acknowledge the influence of my parents and grandparents in shaping my life and my writing.

I would like to thank Mehrdad Mondegari and Kif Anderson for their relentless efforts in putting this book together.

Last and most significantly, I would like to thank all of humanity for keeping my spark as well as my hope alive.

This book is dedicated to:

*My daughter Anahita —
my true teacher of unconditional love.*

*My wife Katayoon —
my true preacher of excellence.*

*My parents and grandparents —
my true treasurers of success.*

*All Humanity who would like to add
Success, Excellence and
Unconditional love in their lives.*

A NON-BELIEVER WROTE

GOD IS NO WHERE

A BELIEVER CHANGED IT TO

GOD IS NOW HERE

The Three Commandments of the
Zoroastrian religion are:

"Good Thoughts, Good Words and Good Deeds"

History shows
Good Thoughts, Good Words and Good Deeds
are truly energized
When we spread so much peace around us,
there is no room for war
When we spread so much love around us,
there is no room for hate
When we spread so much good around us,
there is no room for evil
When we spread so much health around us,
there is no room for sickness
When we spread so much light around us,
there is no room for darkness.

The world
looks lovely
when you look at it
with love
So look at this world
through the eyes
of love.

It doesn't matter
Whether you are a
Vegetarian,
Fruitarian
or
Meatarian
You can always be
A Humanitarian.

Happiness is not in having a family. Happiness is in being a family.

The difference between ordinary and extra-ordinary is that the <u>extra-ordinary know</u> <u>that they can</u> <u>make a difference.</u>

Freedom comes when you <u>free</u> yourself from <u>dom</u>-inating others.

Your hand was designed for reaching out, not pointing out.

When you know
Where you want to go
God will show
The way to go.

*Your net worth
has no value
If it is not built with
your self worth.*

Success
is not in
hitting the headlines.
Success is in
reaching
the heartlines.

Unconditional Love

means

being different

without

becoming indifferent.

When you
work with love
you will
love your work.

Instead of fighting
things in life
Start lighting
things in life.

*Unconditional
love
focuses on
structuring the doing
without
fracturing the being.*

An ideal parent
is the one
who is willing
to learn
from the wisdom
of their children.

Focus on identifying your children instead of rectifying your children.

Parents, use your power to empower your children.

*The only way you will outlive your life.
Is when you will give all your life.*

Silence
has
more power
than
violence.

Life becomes worth living When it's geared towards giving.

Freedom
resides
in your being
not
in your doing.

Create disciplines
that
stretch your life
and
let go of the ones
that
stress your life.

*Your life
will be peaceful
When you give up
your right to be right
For
your right to be happy.*

We truly
forgive and forget
when we
forgive the being
and
forget the doing
not vice versa.

It's only
when you
put your act
together,
that
your act
will
put you together.

Uncommon people
reuse
what
common people
refuse.

There is *no perfection*
in your *doing*
There is *only perfection*
in your *being.*
That's why
we are called
human beings
and not
human doings.

Instead of
guiding your kids
with
strings attached
guide them
with
wings attached.

If we want to develop **E**xtra **N**atural **COURAGE** in our children, We need to **ENCOURAGE** them.

We become kind
when we
unwind the bind
behind our mind.

You can
choose to live
your life in peace
Or you can
choose to live
your life in pieces.

A job makes something for you. A career makes something of you.

In life,
all of our
five senses
will not help
unless we use them
with common sense.

Successful people
have a
lot of latitude
in their attitude.

In dealing
with children,
we do good
when we
pay attention
only to the good.

*Spirituality

comes

when we transform

our barriers of love

into carriers of love.*

Turn your inhibitions into ambitions.

Gratitude should be <u>a part</u> of your attitude, not <u>apart</u> from your attitude.

If you want
to become great
You need
to appreciate—
YOURSELF.

The true test of love

is not

in loving your enemies,

The true test of love

is in not

having any enemies.

**Life is like
a fertilizer
When you spread
what it needs
It will grow
what you want.**

It is better to use your dream and create your touchstone, instead of taking them with you under your tombstone.

We enjoy life

when

we give with passion

and

live with compassion.

**You can always choose
to be peaceful
Even when you
are not joyful.**

Unconditional love creates unity within diversity in humanity.

When you

get to know

That you

always grow

Life becomes

a rainbow.

Meditation

is conformation

of unification

with creation.

Habit is like your shadow
It follows wherever you go
So develop good habits.

Anahita Meher Amalsad
at 2 1/2 years

Every day in every way
I'm growing and glowing.

Anahita Meher Amalsad
at 5 years

Any Thought That Is Focalized Gets Materialized.

Life is a trip that will make you trip. You only enjoy the first trip When you learn from the second.
WOW - WHAT A TRIP!

In life

you either

kiss an opportunity

or

miss an opportunity.

Spirituality
is the
knowing
of
something
in
nothing.

The waves of adversity belong to the ocean of prosperity.

Spiritual

attachment

comes

with

physical

detachment.

You can choose
to work
on your life
or
you can choose
to spend your
lifetime working.
The choice
is yours.

The heart
of your love
comes from
a part
from above.

LIFE

It's a reflection of your expectation.

Put your child
in your
LAP
every day by
practicing the
Love
Appreciation
Pride
principle.

If you don't pay attention Your child will get your attention.

Treat your child

as a co-pilot of a plane

Rather than

as a passenger of a train

Only then

you will get to visit places

far beyond your imagination.

The quest
for earning more
Must be coupled
with the yearning
for learning more.

*Develop attitudes
that exhibit your growth.
And let go of the ones
that inhibit your growth.*

Have

Power
Exhibiting
Action
Creating
Energy

Take

Personal
Responsibility
In
Daily
Effort

Enjoy

Lovely
Instrument
For
Enjoyment

Every day talk about
ITALY and HOLLAND
to the ones
you love
because it stands for:

I Trust And Love You
and
Hope Our Love Lives
And Never Dies

Your personality creates your reality.

*Spiritual consciousness
does not come by
ascending or descending
in life.
Spiritual consciousness
comes only by
transcending in life.*

When dealing with children, practice the art of rubbing out their mistakes instead of rubbing them in.

*We set our life
By the images we get.
But we get our life
By the imaginations we set.*

If your mind
is not offensive
your body
will not be
defensive.

It takes a whole life to develop a whole child.

Meditation

is a

prescription

for

devotion.

Transform your fears or tears into cheers.

**Its only
when we choose
to be open
to everything
That everything
will be open to us.**

It's only when you
begin to work
on you
That everything
will begin
to work
for you.

**Your children
will only
look up to you,
when you
will not
look down on them.**

The true test of parenting
is not in how well
we have learned
to control our children.
The true test of parenting
is in how well
our children have learned
to control themselves.

*When we
give and forgive
Life becomes
fun to live.*

*In life,
you can always
keep things
in control
Without getting
out of control.*

In dealing
with children
be constructive
instead of
being restrictive.

Life becomes productive when we focus on the "Yes" instead of the mess that people create.

Success comes
when we
focus on what's on
and let go
of what's gone.

Include the "right to forgive" in your spiritual constitution.

Tension
peels,
Attention
heals.

Healing comes
when we
focus on the best
and
let go of the rest.

Spirituality
is not in making
the connection,
spirituality
is in being
the connection.

Unconditional love
focuses on
shaping the will
without
shaking the spirit.

*Use
LUV-YA therapy
instead of
psychotherapy.*

Even in the dark,

character shows

Because

it always glows.

FAILURE

It lies in the perception, not in the situation.

*In life
instead of getting
all wired up,
stay
all fired up.*

Spirituality
comes
when we
take the difference
to make a difference
instead of
making attempts
to break the difference.

*Working right
Is more important
Than working smart
or
Working hard.*

We can always be
HUGLY
even when
things look
UGLY.

Our children
need more
"role models"
instead of
"rule models".

The
feeling of healing
comes
when we start
healing the feeling.

**Your words can make people stars
Or leave them with scars.**

Happiness
is followed
When Ego
gets swallowed.

Everyday
do something
to twinkle the eyes
of your
little star.

**When teaching
the love
of truth,
first focus
on the truth
of love.**

Success comes when we analyze our work before we finalize our work.

**When you live
your life
in meditation,
You will have
no need
for medication.**

No love,
No life.
Know love,
Know life.

May the

Light

Of

Valuable

Energy

shine your life
and the life
of all humanity.

What Others Are Saying About This Book

"It's a little book that offers heavy weight words."
The Hanford Sentinel

"The words in this book feel just like reading 'The Prophet'."
Anita Egan Healy
Professional Artist

"The messages in this book remind us that what is in our minds and hearts will be reflected in our bodies and our lives. What an empowering model for creating a life filled with joy."
Suzan Walter
President
American Holistic Health Association

"This book is an extraordinary tool for helping our patients discover the keys to a joyful and healthy life."
Dr. Joyce Johnson
President and Founder
The Wellness Center of California

"The wisdom in this small package can be learned and used for building character and self-esteem in our children."
Dr. Glory Ludwick
Child Psychiatrist and Director
Eldorado School for the Gifted Child

"A pocket teaser of value to people of all faiths."
Rohinton Rivetna
Founding Trustee
Council for the Parliament of World Religions

"This book is packed with thought provoking gems that inspire the heart and rejuvenate the spirit."
FEZANA Journal

INSPIRATION FOR THE HEART
a special excerpt from the book and audio program

LOVE GROWS AND SHOWS ONLY IF IT FLOWS

I have learned some magnificent lessons of unconditional love from my daughter Anahita.

One Day we were famished so we decided to go grab a sandwich from McDonalds. At McDonalds Anahita did something that I did not appreciate, so I decided to bring her back home without buying a sandwich. When we reached home, I thought that she would be really upset with me, instead she told me in a very loving way, **"Baba, you did not get a chance to eat a sandwich at McDonalds. I will make a peanut-butter and jelly sandwich for you so that you don't go hungry."** *This was the first sandwich that she ever made for anybody. I was truly touched by the spirit of her unconditional love and acceptance.*

You see, our children will love us unconditionally when they are young. However, we need to make sure that when they grow up and know better, that we have given them sufficient reasons to continue their unconditional love, and this my friends will only happen when we truly understand, that **the only condition in love is that there are no conditions.**

MOTIVATION FOR THE MIND
a special excerpt from the book and audio program

IN SEARCH OF YOUR QUEST, HOW TO DO YOUR BEST

Success comes when you live your life on a purpose level. Now purpose is not something that you find, purpose is something that you are. Let your purpose outlive you. Create something beautiful for others and give it away for free. Do something so great that even after you're gone, it will continue to touch human lives.

Success is an outcome of a great attitude, success is an offspring of good communication and success is an outgrowth of a worthy purpose. Success is something that you attract by the person you become, and success is living a life that is not only overflowing, but is also everflowing with love.

I want you to keep in mind that in life, no one is better than you, they are just simply ahead of you. And you can also get there if you follow some of the principles of success that we shared with each other today.

For Product Orders, General Sessions,
Seminar Schedules, Keynote Addresses
or Corporate Speaking Inquires

Please contact:

Meher D. Amalsad
15842 Villanova Circle
Westminster, CA 92683
(714) 895-3097

PRODUCTS

AUDIO CASSETTES

• *In Search of Your Quest – How to be Your Best*	*$8.00*
• *Love Grows and Shows Only When it Flows*	*$8.00*

BOOK

• *Gifts That Lift, Shift and Uplift*	*$7.00*
• *Computer screen saver of inspirational quotes*	*$19.95*
• *24 Pack Quotable Business Card Holder*	*$2.99*
• *5 Colorful Gift Stickers of Inspirational Quotes*	*$2.99*
*Shipping and handling charges per item	*$1.00*

SPECIAL BONUS
Buy any three items and
pay no shipping or handling charges.

Delivery Time: 2-4 Weeks

MEHER D. AMALSAD
Professional Speaker, Author & Seminal Leader

For more than a decade, Meher Amalsad had educated, motivated, entertained and influenced the lives of thousands by helping them bring out the best in themselves and in their organizations.

Meher is a published author and an interactive presenter who speaks to Fortune 500 corporations on how to achieve the American Dream. He shares his sensitivity, strength, expressiveness, creativity and intuition, to help others enhance and further develop their potential.

Meher also speaks to professional associations on *"LUV-YA Therapy – Healing Relationships Through Unconditional Love and Forgiveness"*, in which his messages are designed to create unity within diversity in humanity.

Meher is also the author of several best selling audio as well as computer programs. To add to his credits, Meher is featured in *Who's Who Among Rising Americans* and *Who's Who Among Students in American Universities*. He is also a member of various professional speaking organizations.

During Meher's presentations, audiences are required to fasten their seat belts, hold on to their chairs and get ready for an exciting ride.

When looking for an individual who is in touch with himself, with the times and with humanity…

Meher Amalsad is the speaker for all occasions.

The difference between
ALONE and ALL-ONE
is an extra L
which stands for
LOVE, LIGHT and LIFE
When we share our LOVE with others,
we show them the LIGHT
and eventually they become
a part of our LIFE.
That is truly
the transformation
from being ALONE
to becoming ALL-ONE
with humanity.

Thank you for being a part of my
LOVE, LIGHT and LIFE.